CARDIOVASCULAR PATHOPHYSIOLOGY FOR PRE-CLINICAL STUDENTS

DR. ABHISHEK

Contents

Preface

CONTENTS:

Acknowledgements

Acknowledgments

Funding and In-Kind Support

Publication of this work is made possible in part through the support of VIVA (Virtual Library of Virginia), LibreTexts, the Open Education Initiative of the University Libraries at Virginia Tech,

CHAPTER I

Atrial Fibrillation

Atrial fibrillation is the most common cardiac arrhythmia and is caused by rapidly firing potentials in the atrial myocardium. These aberrant depolarizations are often the result of myocardial remodeling and frequently originate within the muscular sleeves that extend into the pulmonary veins from the atria. Causes include hypertension, valvular and ischemic heart disease, and genetics (e.g., mutation of 10q22–q24 on chromosome 10). The rapid depolarizations result in a very fast atrial rate from 400 to 600 bpm. Because the atrial rate is so fast, the ECG shows "coarse fibrillatory waves. the action potentials produced are low amplitude, and P-waves will not be seen.

The rapid atrial depolarizations are transmitted to the atrioventricular (AV) node, but far from all are conducted through to the ventricle because of the node's long refractory period. This means the ventricular rate does not rise to 400–600 bpm (which would be catastrophic), but some of the atrial fibrillation activity can be "lucky" and reach the AV node when it is not in a refractory period. When this occurs, the ventricular rate rises to 100–200 bpm, and QRS complexes can be "irregularly irregular" with a varying R-R interval

Atrial Flutter

Atrial flutter is caused by a macroreentrant current, rather than the multiple sites of aberrant depolarization seen in fibrillation. The cavotricuspid isthmus (CTI) usually provides the circuit for the slower reentrant current to become established (typical atrial flutter), but other sites of reentry and slow conducting circuits are possible (atypical atrial flutter) and are usually associated with structural heart disease or sites of previous surgical or ablations procedures. The slower reentry current produces an atrial rate of 250–350 bpm (compared to the 400–600 of atrial flutter), and P-waves are present but have a characteristic "sawtooth" pattern

CHAPTER II

Heart Failure

While there are numerous pathological causes of heart failure (examples in table 2.1), let us look at how three basic forms of cardiac dysfunction can contribute to impaired cardiac output and congestion. The failing heart may have:

1. Impaired contractility: A decline in contractility is perhaps easiest to visualize; the pumping action of the heart is ineffective/reduced, and blood cannot be cleared from the chambers.

2. An overwhelming afterload: An increased afterload causes the heart to have to work harder to eject blood, and failure to do so leads to poor ejection fractions and cardiac output.

3. Problems with ventricular filling: Impaired ventricular filling during diastole means that the heart has a low preload, but because it cannot pump out what it does not receive, then cardiac output is lower.

For whichever reason the end effect of the failure is a decline in blood flow out of the heart, and consequently congestion on the way in.

Form of dysfunction Example causes

Impaired contractility-

Myocardial infarction

- Coronary atherosclerosis
- Severe anemia
- Cardiomyopathy
- Arrhythmias
- Congenital heart disease

Increased afterload- Severe lung disease

- Hypertension
- Sleep apnea
- Valvular disease

Impaired ventricular filling/relaxation- Cardiomyopathy
- Arrhythmias
- Congenital heart disease
- Valvular disease

Impediments to emptying the heart during systole (i.e., a reduced contractility or increased afterload) were referred to as systolic heart failure. Similarly, problems with filling the ventricle during diastole were referred to as diastolic heart failure.

In reality there is a great deal of overlap between these forms of heart failure, and elements of both can be present in the same patient. Similarly, as both forms result in congestion before the heart and reduced flow after it, they are hard to immediately distinguish. Consequently the type and degree of failure is now categorized by the effect on ejection fraction that can help distinguish the source of the problem.

Heart Failure and Ejection Fraction

Let us quickly remind ourselves of what ejection fraction is. Ejection fraction is the proportion of blood volume that the left ventricle ejects in one beat. It is mathematically described as the starting volume (i.e., end-diastolic volume, EDV) minus the finishing volume (i.e., end-systolic volume, ESV) as a proportion of the starting volume —in simpler terms, what percentage of the ventricular blood volume was pushed out during a contraction.

Ejection Fraction in Systolic Failure

Let us first relate this to systolic failure by looking at what happens when the contractility of the myocardium is reduced. In systolic failure, there is a problem getting blood out of the heart, so the volume of blood coming out of the heart per beat (EDV-ESV) is reduced. However, the end diastolic volume will remain the same, or more likely rise. So our ejection fraction is reduced. Consequently, if you have a reduced ejection fraction you know you have a systolic failure. So to improve diagnosis, systolic failure is now referred to as heart failure with a reduced ejection fraction (HFREF).

Let us look at the pathophysiological consequences of HFREF. With a poor ejection fraction blood will begin to accumulate in the ventricle, and EDV will begins to rise and consequently so will the ventricular pressure. The raised pressure will impede venous return and promote venous congestion as blood struggles to enter the heart, and in the case of left ventricular failure the congestion will occur first in the left atrium and then in the pulmonary system.

So systolic failure is referred to as HFREF, but what started as a problem emptying the heart has led to congestion and has produced a problem getting blood into the heart. Let us compare this with diastolic failure.

Ejection Fraction in Diastolic Failure

Remember that in diastolic failure there is a problem relaxing/filling the ventricle. Consequently EDV tends to be lower than normal, and this lower volume of blood in the chamber is relatively easy for the heart to expel. So proportionately, the ejection fraction can be maintained, even if the absolute stroke volume may be low. This is now classified as heart failure with a normal ejection fraction (HFNEF).

The pathophysiological consequences of HFNEF stem from the poor relaxation of the ventricle and/or ability to accept blood. When the ventricle is noncompliant during diastole (i.e., does not relax properly), it does not take much blood volume to enter the chamber before the ventricle pressure begins to rise. This rise in ventricular pressure opposes the entry of more blood, so it accumulates in the atrium. Atrial pressure rises and venous return is impeded, so blood becomes congested in the venous system.

If you compare this sequence of events in HFREF and HFNEF in figure 2.3 the end point is the same—congestion in the venous system, hence the difficulty in distinguishing "systolic" and "diastolic" failure and the need to measure ejection fraction and the newer categories of HFREF and HFNEF. In summary, HFREF starts with a problem getting blood out, that leads to a problem getting blood in, whereas HFNEF starts with a problem getting blood in that leads to a problem getting blood out. Both produce congestion, and both result in a diminished cardiac output.

Acute Responses to Reduced Cardiac Output in Heart Failure: Good or Bad?

Initial responses to the diminished cardiac output include the acute compensatory responses to low blood pressure, myocardial stretch, or changes in renal perfusion. Let us do a quick review.

The reduced cardiac output leads to a reduced arterial blood pressure, which, in combination with low volume exiting the heart, results in lower blood flow. With less blood exiting the heart, more remains in the chamber, particularly with systolic failure, so the myocardium is stretched. These three factors (pressure, flow, and myocardial stretch) elicit mechanical, neural, and hormone responses intended to correct the fall in pressure, resume flow, and clear the heart of congestion—but these responses are intended for a normal heart, not one undergoing failure.

First, the extended myocardium elicits the Frank-Starling mechanism to increase contractility, while the release of ANP and BNP induces sodium and fluid loss at the kidney. Conversely, reduced renal blood flow instigates the RAAS system to cause salt and fluid retention and vasoconstriction aided by the release of Endothelin-1 from the endothelium of flow-deprived vessels. Finally, the reduced arterial pressure prompts the baroreceptor reflex that increases sympathetic tone to increase rate and contractility, and antidiuretic hormone causes fluid retention.

These compensatory effects are all attempts to improve cardiac output and blood pressure, but the failing heart is being forced to work harder against an increased afterload and move more volume. Consequently, but for the natriuretic peptides, these responses are maladaptive in the long term, and chronic changes to the heart are instigated.

Chronic Remodeling and Hypertrophy

Volume overload increases preload and consequently the chamber radius. Laplace's law states that this larger radius means the chamber wall must generate more tension to contain the same chamber pressure.

Pressure overload creates higher demands to generate greater pressures to overcome an increased afterload. This requires additional wall tension and also leads to hypertrophy.

But the two forms of overload (volume and pressure) lead to different patterns of hypertrophy. In volume overload the myocytes add more sarcomeres in series, so they elongate and contribute to the dilation of the chamber while there is a proportional increase in wall thickness. This is referred to as eccentric hypertrophy

Pressure loading, on the other hand, leads to the synthesis of new sarcomeres that are formed in parallel to the old ones, causing an increase in wall thickness without any dilation of the chamber. This is referred to as concentric hypertrophy (figure 2.5).

Figure 2.6: Normal myocardial (A) and myocardium exposed to valvular disease (B).

These adaptations are accompanied by increased deposition of connective tissue that may have conductive or contractive ramifications. The difference in myocytic arrangement and presence of connective tissue is clear in the histological views of normal myocardium and myocardium chronically exposed to valvular disease in figure 2.6.

Myocytes may also be lost through either apoptosis or necrosis. As hypertrophy occurs the blood supply to the thickening wall becomes inadequate so infarction and consequent necrosis are more likely. Factors that promote myocyte apoptosis are all present during heart failure and include elevated catecholamines, Angiotensin II, inflammatory cytokines, and wall stress.

These same factors also disrupt gene expression in myocytes and cause intracellular deficits, including loss of Ca++ homeostasis and production of high-energy phosphates. While the mechanisms of these intracellular effects is still being heavily researched, the inability to control calcium or regulate high-energy phosphates obviously has implications of excitation–contraction coupling.

So while hypertrophy may seem a sensible response in the failing heart, the patterns and inflammation and stress-driven changes are eventually maladaptive and lead to a progressive decline in cardiac function.

Clinical Manifestations of Heart Failure

If the right heart fails, there is a rise in systemic venous pressure and peripheral edema arises. There may be abdominal discomfort as the liver becomes engorged and a loss of appetite or nausea as gastrointestinal edema arises. If the left heart fails, then the pulmonary circulation is exposed to the congestion and pulmonary edema arises.

Low cardiac output reduces renal filtration, so urine formation maybe impaired. Similarly cerebral blood flow may be compromised, causing dulled mental status.

Orthopnea arises when the patient lays down and venous return toward the failing left ventricle increases, compounding the pulmonary congestion. Patients often sleep propped up on pillows to elevate the heart and lungs. In severe cases the patient may only be able to sleep upright in a chair.

CHAPTER III

Hypertension

Over seventy million Americans are hypertensive, and the Framingham study suggests that 90 percent of those over fifty-five years old will develop hypertension. But two-thirds of hypertensive patients are unaware of their condition so are exposed to the long-term effects.

The current guidelines (JNC 8, 2017) list the following pressures and categories to define hypertension:

Normal (<120/80 mm Hg)
Elevated (120–129/<80 mm Hg)
Stage 1 hypertension (130–139/80–89 mm Hg)
Stage 2 hypertension (≥140/90 mm Hg)

Essential Hypertension

Hypertension can be categorized as either essential or secondary. Secondary is much less common and a consequence of another condition (e.g., renal or endocrine disease). Essential hypertension (EH), despite being the prevalent form, is poorly understood but can be attributed to a problem with either cardiac output or peripheral resistance (i.e., the components of blood pressure regulation). Because multiple factors contribute to these components AND there is evidence of some genetic component to hypertension AND due to the contribution from environmental factors, essential hypertension can be considered a "description" rather than a "diagnosis." Primary abnormalities that may contribute to essential hypertension are shown in figure 3.1.

Genetic components of essential hypertension

No single loci has been identified as causing hypertension, but strong familial histories suggest polygenic causes (i.e., multiple loci are involved). Much attention has been paid to genes involved with enzymes and receptor production within the Renin-Angiotensin-Aldosterone (RAA) system because of its critical role in blood pressure control through sodium and volume regulation. Similarly genes involved with renal regulation of sodium have been studied. Our inability to demonstrate a genetic basis to hypertension is also consistent with significant environmental causes.

Systemic abnormalities and EH

Since Blood Pressure = Cardiac Output x Peripheral Resistance, it should be easy to imagine why aberrant rises in cardiac output (e.g., increased sympathetic tone) or peripheral resistance (e.g., low levels of vasodilators) would cause a rise in blood pressure (BP). Some of those aberrations of the acute BP control mechanisms , but this is clearly half the story as there are chronic control mechanisms that should surely compensation for loss of acute control. What this means is, for hypertension to be sustained, the kidney must be "in on the hypertension act." While the kidney itself can be responsible for volume-based hypertension (dysregulated renal blood flow, ion channels defects, etc.), there are deficits in renal control in hypertension. Renin levels are normal or high in 70 to 75 percent of EH patients—and of course they should be low as elevated BP should suppress renin secretion. So while this begins a chicken-and-egg scenario, for hypertension to be sustained, both acute and chronic control mechanisms must fail.

Diabetes, obesity, and EH

The linkage between diabetes and EH, and obesity and EH, appears strong and direct. Because insulin is a dietary-induced mediator of sympathetic activity, the elevated insulin levels in insulin-resistant diabetes can directly promote hypertension. Insulin can also lead to an increase in peripheral resistance via its mitogenic effect on vascular smooth muscle that causes hypertrophy in the medial vascular layers and a decrease in lumen size.

Obesity can also induce hypertension through release of angiotensinogen from more abundant adipocytes, thus providing more substrate for the RAA system. The increase in body mass is also accompanied by an increase in blood volume, and that blood may be more viscous as the large population of adipocytes release coagulative proteins, including prothrombin.

Secondary Hypertension

Although not as common, there are numerous causes of secondary hypertension. There are some distinguishing features that are clinically useful to distinguish it from EH. Your first heads-up is if the patient is younger and not in the typical range for EH (> fifty years old). Secondary hypertension also tends to be more severe, and BP can rise dramatically; EH does not have a rapid onset. While EH often comes with family history, secondary hypertension is more sporadic.

Suspicion of secondary hypertension can usually be confirmed by urinalysis that reveals the underlying issue (see table 3.1 for some common causes and cues for diagnosis). Disturbances in electrolytes and creatinine accompany the renal and mineralocorticoid-based diseases. Pheochromocytoma is rare and accounts for 0.2 percent of secondary hypertension cases (however, it is much more common in exam questions than it is in the clinic!).

Drugs that disrupt the angiotensinogen pathways (e.g., estrogens), are sympathomimetic (e.g., over-the-counter cold remedies), or promote sodium and water retention (e.g., NSAIDS) can all produce secondary hypertension.

Primary disorderClinical cues

Chronic renal disease- Increased creatinine

- Abnormal urinalysis

Primary aldosteronism- Decreased serum potassium

Renovascular- Abdominal bruit

- Sudden onset
- Decreased serum potassium

Pheochromocytoma- Palpitations, diaphoresis, headache, weight loss

- Episodic hypertension

Coarctation of the aorta- Blood pressure in arms > legs

- Blood pressure in right arm > left arm
- Midsystolic click

Cushing syndrome- Central obesity

- Hirsutism

Consequences of Hypertension

As most hypertensive patients are asymptomatic, the condition can be left unmanaged and allowed to produce significant chronic effects. Most of these effects are caused by the extra work placed on the heart with the increased afterload and the damage to the interior of the vasculature.

The excess afterload can lead to systolic dysfunction and eventually heart failure with reduced ejection fraction (HFREF). In response to the excessive afterload the left ventricle can hypertrophy, causing a loss of compliance diastolic dysfunction and eventually heart failure with normal ejection fraction (HFNEF). The increased workload and muscle mass also increase the myocardial oxygen demand. This increase in demand often occurs at the same time that blood supply is diminished by concurrent atherosclerosis that is accelerated by the hypertension-induced arterial damage. Consequently, with high demand and low supply, the patient is prone to ischemia and myocardial infarction.

The arterial damage will also promote thrombosis and atheroemboli, so risk of embolic stroke is raised. Risk of hemorrhagic stroke is also increased as the vessel ways become weak. The large vessels are also at risk of being unable to counteract raised pressure (remember Laplace's law?), so aortic aneurysm and dissection can also occur.

High pressures entering the renal circulation can lead to nephrosclerosis. As renal function declines, a vicious cycle forms with renal failure exacerbating hypertension that exacerbates renal failure.

The retinal circulation provides a direct window into the state of the vasculature. Rapid onset and severe hypertension may burst small retinal vessels and produce local infarctions. In more chronic cases, arterial narrowing and medial hypertrophy of the retinal vessel can be seen. As the chronic hypertension worsens, arterial sclerosis is evident. While these chronic effects may not produce functional issues, they are at least an accessible indicator of the vascular status.

Hypertensive Crisis

Most commonly caused by a hemodynamic insult overlaid on chronic hypertension, a hypertensive crisis is a severe elevation of blood pressure that can become life threatening through raising intracranial pressure. The rise in intracranial pressure produces severe headache, blurred vision, confusion, or even coma and is referred to as hypertensive encephalopathy. Funduscopy reveals retinal hemorrhages, exudates, and sometimes papilledema. The massive afterload on the left ventricle can precipitate angina. Therapy must be rapid to prevent permanent vascular consequences, and if administered in time the acute changes are usually reversed. However, the underlying cause of the crisis (usually renal failure) will persist.

CHAPTER IV

Valvular Disease

In basic terms, normal valves maintain normal direction of blood flow through the heart's chambers. If they do not close properly they can allow backflow (regurgitation). If the valve does not fully open or is narrowed (stenosed), then the raised resistance impedes blood movement on its normal route and extra propulsive force must be applied by the myocardium. The clinical manifestations of cardiac valve disease vary depending on the valve involved, the form of dysfunction, and the severity and rate of onset of that dysfunction.

Abnormalities of valvular structure and/or function can either be congenital or acquired. Acquired valvular disease is by far the most common and is most prevalent in the elderly. The high blood flow and pressures that valves are exposed to make them particularly susceptible to other risk factors that promote valvular damage (see table 4.1). Congenital valvular defects arise from disrupted heart development, about 50 percent of which involve the valves. The impact of congenital defects has diminished with the advent of advanced detection techniques. What we will spend time on in this chapter is the main instigating factors and pathologies that result in acquired valvular defects.

Risk factors

Age

Gender

Tobacco use

Hypercholesterolemia

Rheumatic heart disease

Hypertension

Type II diabetes

Pathophysiology of Valvular Disease

The constant stress of facing high flow and pressure over thirty to forty million cardiac contractions a year is not without its consequences, and the most common valvular disorder is calcification that comes with "wear-and-tear" and aging. The presence of other factors such as hyperlipidemia, hypertension, and inflammation accelerate this process and promote the deposition of hydroxyapatite (a form of calcium phosphate), and the valve structure contains cells that resemble osteoblasts.

As they face the most pressure, the aortic and mitral valves are more prone to calcification. The most common pattern of calcification in the aortic valve is mounded masses within the cusps of the valve that eventually fuse and stop the valve from opening fully. Calcification in the mitral valve tends to start in the fibrous annulus, which does not impact valvular function to the same extent, but in exceptional cases can cause regurgitation or stenosis, or even arrhythmias as calcium deposits impinge on the atrioventricular conduction system .

ValveDeposition of calciumGross pathConsequences

AorticCuspStenosis

MitralAnnulus- Stenosis

- Regurgitation
- Arrhythmias

Mitral Valve Prolapse (MVP)

A prolapsed mitral valve is one where one or both leaflets have become floppy and capable of ballooning back into the left atrium during systole (. The condition is more common in women, affects 2–3 percent of adults in the United States, and can be a secondary effect of mitral valve regurgitation.

The causes of MVP are usually unidentified, but a few cases can be attributed to inherited connective tissue disorders such as Marfan syndrome. The prolapsed valve leaflet composition is enlarged and thickened with deposition of myxomatous material rich in proteoglycans, and a reduction in the structurally critical fibrosa layer where a higher prevalence of type III collagen (a more stretchy than structural form of collagen) is found.

The flapping valve structure can cause secondary fibrosis on the structures it strikes, such as the leaflet edges or the endocardium where the abnormally elongated cords rub. The agitation may also promote thrombus formation in the atrium.

The resultant floppy leaflet can be detected by a midsystolic click, and any associated incompetence may produce a late-systolic murmur . MVP is usually asymptomatic, but potential complications include:

A propensity for endocardial infection,
An increased risk of regurgitation and cord rupture,
An increased stroke risk, and
Higher incidence of arrhythmias.

Rheumatic Heart Disease

Rheumatic heart disease (RHD) is virtually the only cause of mitral valve stenosis. It arises after a group A streptococcal infection that often originates in the upper airway and leads to rheumatic fever (a multisystem, immune-mediated disease). The incidence in developed countries is relatively low because of rapid diagnosis and treatment of the instigating pharyngitis, but in poor, crowed, urban areas RHD remains an important health issue.

The acute results of rheumatic fever occur days to weeks after the streptococcal infection, and while the initial pharyngeal infection may have cleared and the test results have become negative, the antibodies to the streptococcal enzymes (Streptolysin O and DNase B) can still be detected. The initial cardiac effects include carditis, pericardial rubs, tachycardia, and arrhythmias. However, the chronic effects may arise years or even decades later.

The chronic effects involve an immune cross-reaction between the antibodies and CD4+ T-cells directed against the streptococcal

M proteins and cardiac self-antigens. Antibody binding and T-cell activity toward the cardiac antigens activate complement and recruit neutrophils and macrophages toward the valve tissue. The damage they produce includes histologically distinct lesions called Aschoff bodies (figure 4.3), and plump activated macrophages called Anitschkow cells (or caterpillar cells) appear in the effected areas . All layers of the myocardium can be effected, but the valves can show leaflet thickening and fusion as well as shortened, thickened cords. Vegetative verrucae are associated with the necrotic fibrinoid foci, making RHD one of the vegetative forms of valvular disease.

As the valve thickens it can become calcified as well, and the adhered leaflets produce a “fish-mouth” or “button hole” appearance that causes the valve to narrow. The damage is cumulative with the increased turbulence through a stenosed valve perpetuating the fibrotic process (see summary in figure 4.3).

Infective Endocarditis

Infective endocarditis (IE) is divided into acute and subacute forms, depending on the virulence of the causal pathogen. Acute IE is rapid in onset and involves highly destructive pathogens that cause necrosis and significant lesions that can lead to death in a matter of days. Subacute IE, alternatively, can deform the valves over weeks to months and generally involves a much less destructive pathogen.

Acute cases tend to involve healthy individuals and are responsible for 20 to 30 percent of cases, whereas the less virulent pathogens that cause subacute IE tend to need a foothold and only affect previously damaged or deformed valves.

Most incidence of IE start with fever, but it can also manifest as nonspecific fatigue, weight loss, or flu-like symptoms in older adults. The infection leads to vegetations on the valve that are the hallmark of IE . These lesions contain fibrin, inflammatory cells, and bacteria.

The risk is twofold as the vegetations can:

Disrupt valve function and form abscesses into the underlying myocardium, and

Embolize and carry the pathogens to a new septic infarcts or obstruct vasculature.

After a few weeks, complications arise that are the product of immune complex deposition or emboli. They can include glomerulonephritis as immune complexes become embedded in the glomerular basement membrane. Other later complications are now rare due to early detection and effective treatment but can include microthromboemboli that produce splinter or subungual lesions. Other hemorrhagic signs include Janeway lesions on the palms or soles, Osler nodes on the fingers, or Roth spots on the retina

Noninfective Vegetations

Some vegetations are sterile (i.e., occur in the absence of infection). There are two main examples of this—nonbacterial thrombotic endocarditis (NBTE) and the systemic lupus erythematosus (SLE).

Figure 4.6: NBTE with small thrombi binding to valve leaflets.

Often coinciding with emboli in other sites, NBTE occurs in states of hypercoagulability, such as in cancer or sepsis. The small thrombi (1–5 mm) bind to the valve leaflets (figure 4.6), but do not illicit an inflammatory response nor are they invasive. Often the local consequences are trivial, but they can be the source of emboli that lead to infarcts in the brain, heart, or elsewhere.

In SLE, the vegetations are again sterile and small (1–4 mm) with a pink, wart-like appearance that are composed of eosinophilic material, granular material, and cellular debris. They tend to adhere to the undersurfaces of the atrioventricular valves, the valvular endocardium, and the cords (figure 4.7). Unlike NBTE, the vegetations can instigate complement and Fc-bearing cells that cause intense valvulitis. The end product of this is referred to as Libman Sacks disease.

Carcinoid Heart Disease

Lastly, carcinoid heart disease is the cardiac manifestation of carcinoid syndrome. Carcinoid tumors are neuroendocrine tumors that usually arise in the gastrointestinal tract or lungs, and they secrete a number of mediators (figure 4.8) that can give rise to carcinoid heart disease.

The liver normally metabolizes these circulating mediators, but when the metastatic burden overwhelms hepatic clearance, the right heart is exposed to their effects (the left heart is somewhat protected by the degradation performed by the pulmonary circulation).

Of all these released mediators, serotonin is the most likely candidate for causing cardiac effects, although the mechanism is not clear. Once established, carcinoid lesions are distinctive white intimal thickenings (figure 4.8) composed of smooth muscle cells and collagen embedded in a mucopolysaccharide matrix. The most common manifestations are tricuspid insufficiency and pulmonary stenosis.

CHAPTER V

Heart Sounds and Murmurs

As unintrusive as the ECG is, listening to the heart is a cheap, quick, and informative clinical test. We will cover the basic structure, causes, and common pathologies of heart murmurs as a companion guide to clinical skills classes on auscultation of the chest. A good understanding of the cardiac cycle would be beneficial.

Heart Sounds

The first and second sounds (S1 and S2) are the fundamental heart sounds.

S1 occurs at the beginning of isovolumetric contraction. The ventricle is beginning to contract, so ventricular pressure quickly rises above atrial pressure and the atrioventricular (tricuspid and mitral) valves close, producing the S1 sound. The mitral valve normally closes slightly (0.04 seconds) before the tricuspid, causing S1 to be "split" (i.e., actually being two sounds, M1 and T . but the time gap is too short with a normal heart to be detectable with a stethoscope. The reasons for M1 preceding T1 are not clear, but may be due to the force generation of the left ventricle being slightly faster than that of the right ventricle. The splitting of S1 can be more pronounced and audible in the presence of a right bundle branch block that causes left ventricular contraction (and mitral valve closure) to markedly precede contraction of the right ventricle. Conversely, in the case of a left bundle branch block, the normal splitting of S1 may be absent as M1 is delayed and so occurs in synchrony with T1.

S2 is caused by closure of the aortic and pulmonic valves at the beginning of isovolumetric ventricular relaxation when ventricular pressure falls below pulmonary and aortic pressure. As aortic pressure (80 mmHg) is far greater than pulmonary artery pressure

(10 mmHg), S2 is normally split with two components (A2 and P2) relating to the closure of the aortic and pulmonic valves, respectively. How split A2 and P2 are depend on physiological conditions, primarily the phase of breathing that influences the pulmonary artery pressure. In expiration pulmonary artery pressure is higher, so the pulmonic valve closes earlier and P2 occurs closer to A2. Conversely, during inspiration pulmonary artery pressure falls, so pulmonic valve closing occurs later and A2 and P2 occur further apart (figure 5.2). This physiological splitting can be heard with a stethoscope, but can be further influenced by diseases as listed in table 5.1.

Changes in S2 splitting and possible underlying causes

Abnormally wide splitting- Right ventricle (RV) volume overload (e.g., atrial septal defect)
- RV outflow obstruction (e.g., pulmonary stenosis)
- RBBB

Narrow splitting- Pulmonary hypertension
- Mild to moderate aortic stenosis

Single S2- One semilunar valve is absent (e.g., truncus arteriosus, valvular atresia)
- Large ventricular septal defect (equal ventricular pressures)
- Pulmonary hypertension with equal ventricular pressures

Paradoxical splitting (P2 before A2)- Severe aortic stenosis
- LBBB

S3 is associated with the rapid filling phase of the ventricle (when the AV valves open), about 0.14 to 0.16 seconds after S2 (closure of the aortic and pulmonic valves). The exact cause of the sound is unclear, but a normal S3 occurs as a brief, low-frequency vibration. Previously thought to be an intracardiac sound arising from vibrations in the valve cusps or ventricular wall, more recent studies suggest the sound may be due to the filling ventricular wall hitting the inner chest wall, or it may arise from the ventricular apex as it hits a limitation of its longitudinal expansion.

Common causes of abnormal S3

Dilated cardiomyopathy

Chronic mitral valve regurgitation
Diastolic heart failure
Pregnancy (not pathological sign)
Athletes (not pathological sign)

As S3 is a filling sound, an abnormal S3 (higher pitch and referred to as a ventricular gallop) is an important clue to heart failure or volume overload (see table 5.2). The absence of an abnormal S3 does not rule out heart failure, but its presence is a sensitive indicator of ventricular dysfunction. Constriction around the heart (e.g., constrictive pericarditis) may cause an early S3, or "pericardial knock."

S4 is abnormal and is associated with poor ventricular compliance (e.g., ventricular hypertrophy). It occurs during atrial contraction and is associated with the atrial pressure pulse. The sound is thought to be caused by reverberation of the stiffened ventricular wall as blood is propelled into the ventricle from the atrium (hence it is also known as an atrial gallop). S4 and raised end-diastolic ventricular pressure (EDVP) commonly occur together as both are caused by poor ventricular compliance, so S4 tends to be associated with conditions that cause pressure overload (see table 5.3).

Common causes of abnormal S4
Hypertensive heart disease
Aortic stenosis
Hypertrophic cardiomyopathy
Acute phase of myocardial infarction
Acute and severe mitral or aortic regurgitation

Ejection Sounds (Clicks)

As S1 and S2 occur during closure of heart valves, pathological conditions can lead to the valves producing a high-frequency "clicking" sound when they open during chamber ejection—hence they can be referred to as ejection sounds and they are pathological.

Aortic ejection sounds usually occur 0.12–0.14 seconds after the Q-wave of the ECG (i.e., after ventricular pressure has risen to exceed aortic pressure). Because of its timing, the "click" produced can be misinterpreted as a split S1. The abnormal opening of the aortic valve is usually caused by a deformed but mobile valve leaflet or aortic root dilation that may be caused by the conditions.

Pulmonary ejection sounds occur a little earlier (0.09–0.11 seconds) after the Q-wave as the pulmonary valve opens a little earlier. It can also be distinguished by the fact that its intensity is diminished during inspiration as increased venous return during inspiration augments the effect of atrial contraction and causes a "gentler" opening of the valve. As with the aortic ejection sounds, pulmonary ejection sounds are associated with deformed valves or pulmonary arterial dilation.

A click occurring in diastole is associated with abnormal opening of either the mitral or tricuspid valve. Similar to systolic clicks, a diastolic click can be misinterpreted as a split S2. The most common cause of diastolic clicks is valvular stenosis of an AV valve.

AorticPulmonary

- Aortic stenosis
- Bicuspid aortic valve
- Aortic regurgitation
- Aneurysm in ascending aorta- Pulmonary stenosis
- Pulmonary arterial dilation
- Pulmonary hypertension

Heart Murmurs

A murmur is the sound of turbulence associated with abnormal blood flow through a valve or chamber. The turbulent flow produces low-frequency audible sounds that are distinct from heart sounds associated with valve closures. Murmurs can be divided into those caused by valvular defects and those caused by abnormal interchamber flow. Depending on the defect involved, the murmur may occur during diastole and systole, hence distinguishing whether a murmur is diastolic or systolic is a useful first diagnostic step.

Classification of a murmur includes the intensity (Grades 1–6, faintest to loudest), the pitch (high or low), configuration, location, and timing. The timing refers to the onset and duration of the murmur, and the classifications are shown in table 5.5 with some common causes listed there and below.

Aortic stenosis produces a midsystolic murmur that has a crescendo–decrescendo pattern (intensity builds up, then fades). This pattern relates to the level of turbulent flow through the narrowed valve—slow at first as the resistance is overcome, then fading away as blood flow decreases.

Mitral/tricuspid regurgitation produces a holosystolic murmur as the incompetent valve allows a constant turbulent (and reverse) flow from the ventricle back to the atria.

Mitral valve prolapse produces a late-systolic murmur often proceeded by a midsystolic click. The click is caused by tensioning of the chordae tendineae as ventricular pressure increases and the murmur builds up as regurgitation is established.

Ventricular septal defect produces a holosystolic murmur when severe. Turbulent flow through the defect is constant as the left ventricular pressure is higher than right ventricular pressure throughout systole—hence a continuous left–right shunt is established.

Aortic regurgitation produces a "blowing" diastolic murmur that is usually decrescendo. This early diastolic murmur is short because rapidly rising ventricular pressure (due to atrial and aortic contributions) ends the reverse flow from the aorta. In cases when the aortic pressure is high, the regurgitation may be sustained and the murmur becomes pandiastolic.

Mitral stenosis produces a diastolic murmur that starts late as the stenosed valve prevents atria-to-ventricular flow until high atrial pressures are established. The murmur may be preceded by a middiastolic click as the atrial pressure finally "flings" the valve open.

CHAPTER VI

Congenital Heart Disease

In this chapter we will look at congenital heart diseases on a disease-by-disease basis. It might also be useful to review your heart embryology as it is highly relevant to the defects we will be looking at.

Atrial Septal Defect (ASD)

Embryology

The most common atrial septal defects arise from:

Failure of the osteum secundum (most common),

Excessive resorption of the septum primum, or

Failure of septum primum to fuse with endocardial cushions (less common).

A patent foramen ovale (20 percent of the population) is not a true ASD as no tissue is missing and the remaining tissue acts as a one-way valve, so a PFO does not have the same pathophysiology as a true ASD. ASDs are common in infants with Down syndrome, as are VSDs.

Pathophysiology

ASDs allow blood flow between the atria. As the pressure in the left atria is higher than that in the left, blood flows from left to right (figure 6.1). This causes volume overload of the right side of the heart. This excessive load may lead to right ventricular compliance being reduced as remodeling takes place. The reduced compliance can elevate right-side pressure and thereby reduce the left–right shunt.

Ventricular Septal Defect (VSD)

Embryology

Most ventricular septal defects arise from membraneous portion of the septum (70 percent), while others form in the muscular portion (20 percent); less frequently they occur near the aortic or AV valves.

Pathophysiology

The manifestations of a VSD depend on the VSD size and the relative resistance of the pulmonary and systemic circulations—all of which will determine the direction of blood flow. During fetal development, the pulmonary and systemic circulations have equivalent resistances, so there may be very little shunting through the VSD, particularly if it is small. After birth, however, the resistance of the pulmonary system falls dramatically, so right ventricular pressure is lower and below left ventricular pressure (which still has to contend with systemic resistance)—consequently a left–right shunt is established. If this shunt is large (depending on the size of the defect), then blood returning from the pulmonary circulation to the left atrium can pass into the left ventricle, through the VSD into the right ventricle and head back into pulmonary circulation to start this loop again .

When a large VSD is present, the recirculated blood causes volume overload of the right ventricle and the pulmonary circulation and subsequently both chambers of the left heart (figure 6.2). This can eventually cause chamber dilation and lead to heart failure. The extra volume load in the pulmonary circulation can also lead to early onset of pulmonary vascular disease.

Coarctation of the Aorta

Embryology

Coarctation of the aorta (figure 6.3) is a constriction of the aortic lumen, usually close to the ductus. The cause is unclear, but low flow through the left heart and aorta flow during development may cause the defect (no flow, no grow).

Pathophysiology

The diminished lumen causes increased afterload on the left ventricle. Vessels branching off the aorta before the coarctation can receive normal blood flow, so the head (carotid) and upper extremities (subclavian) are usually properly perfused whereas branching arteries after the coarctation may be underperfused. Consequently, differential cyanosis is a possible manifestation.

Tetralogy of Fallot (ToF)

Embryology

In Tetralogy of Fallot (ToF) the outflow tract (infundibular) portion of the interventricular septum is displaced. This single defect leads to four defects:

Subvalvular pulmonic stenosis, because of the displaced infundibular septum (#1, figure 6.4),

Right ventricular hypertrophy caused by the pulmonic stenosis ,

VSD—caused by malalignment of the interventricular septum , and

Overriding aorta that receives blood from both ventricles .

Other defects can be associated with ToF, but the defects listed above lead this to be the most common form of cyanotic congenital heart disease.

Pathophysiology

The high resistance of the stenosed pulmonic valve (#1, figure 6.4) causes the blood in the right ventricle to exit through VSD (#3, figure 6.4) and enter the left ventricle forming a right-left shunt, bypassing the pulmonary circulation. Consequently blood with venous PO2 enters the systemic circulation and hypoxemia/cyanosis results. The degree of hypoxemia/cyanosis that occurs depends on the degree of pulmonic stenosis.

Transposition of the Great Arteries

Embryology

Although not completely understood, it is thought that failure of the aortic-pulmonary septum to spiral during development results in the great vessels coming off the wrong ventricles—the aorta exits the right, and the pulmonary artery exits the left. Other theories exist.

Pathophysiology

The placement of the pulmonary artery on the left means left ventricular blood is pumped up to pulmonary circulation, only to return to the left side of the heart via the pulmonary veins. Similarly, the aorta on the right forms a closed-system with the right ventricle pumping into the systemic circulation, only for it to return to the right atrium via the vena cava (see figure 6.5). So how is this compatible with life? In short, it is not. Embryonic development can continue because the two looped circulations can mix at the ductus arteriosus and foramen ovale of the fetal circulation. But after birth these shunts between the two circulations MUST be artificially maintained, or the patient must be "fortunate" enough to also have a VSD for mixing to take place.

Patent Ductus Arteriosus

Embryology

The ductus arteriosus is part of the fetal circulation allowing blood in the pulmonary artery to bypass the nonfunctional, high resistance lungs and instead traverse into the aorta and systemic circulation. The ductus should close at birth, and failure to do so leaves a patent ductus arteriosus (PDA).

Pathophysiology

In utero, the high resistance of the pulmonary circulation ensures that blood is diverted through the ductus arteriosis into the aorta. However, at birth there is a dramatic fall in the resistance of the pulmonary circulation as the lungs inflate. The pressure gradient across the ductus is consequently reversed (low on the pulmonary side, high on the systemic), so if the ductus remains open blood will flow from the aorta to the pulmonary artery (i.e., the opposite direction to fetal circulation) (figure 6.6).

The consequences of this are that a greater volume of blood reenters the pulmonary circulation, the left atria, and the left ventricle. Consequently the compartments of the left heart can eventually fail through volume overload. When the left heart fails, the shunt through the PDA can be reversed, and desaturated blood destined for the pulmonary circulation can end up passing through the PDA to the aorta instead—this reversal later in life is called Eisenmenger syndrome. In Eisenmenger's the upper extremities receive uncontaminated, saturated blood, as their branching arteries are upstream of the desaturated blood entering the aorta at the PDA. Not so for the lower extremities whose arteries branch after the PDA and so receive low oxygen blood. Hence in Eisenmenger syndrome patients, only the feet are cyanosed.

Atrioventricular Canal

Embryology

Complete AV canal defect is a result of complete failure of fusion between endocardial cushions. It is characterized by a primum atrial septal defect (#1, figure 6.7) that is contiguous with a ventricular septal defect (#4 in figure 6.7) and a malformed or common AV valve. Although several forms of this defect exist, this complete form is effectively a single chambered heart.

Pathophysiology

The malformed valves allow regurgitation, and the unrestricted interventricular communication allow a profound left–right shunt. This leads to volume overload in the pulmonary circulation, and heart failure will be produced if there is no correction. Pulmonary artery hypertension (PAH) and premature development of pulmonary vascular obstructive disease are other common outcomes.

Truncus Arteriosus

Embryology

Failed development of the truncoconal septum that normally leads to separation of the pulmonary artery and aorta leads to truncus arteriosus (TA). This condition leads to a single vessel with a single (often incompetent) valve positioned above the ventricular septum
.

Pathophysiology

The underlying issues with TA are 1) mixing of blood from the left (saturated) and right heart (unsaturated), and 2) the common valve can allow regurgitation. In utero the high pulmonary vascular resistance means most blood exiting the heart goes through the aorta and cardiac output is rarely affected. At birth mild cyanosis can be produced by the mixing of blood from the left and right heart, but as pulmonary vascular resistance remains high in the first few days of life, cardiac output my be maintained. As pulmonary vascular resistance continues to fall in the first few weeks of life, a significant left–right shunt can become established as more left ventricular blood finds it "easier" to ascend up the pulmonary artery. Similar to a VSD, this leads to volume overload in the pulmonary circulation and eventually heart failure. The heart failure has a more rapid onset in TA than VSD if the common valve allows regurgitation. The regurgitation lowers end-diastolic ventricular volumes, so cardiac work to maintain cardiac output increases and promotes myocardial ischemia. Add to this the left–right shunt (as seen in VSD) and heart failure is more likely.

CHAPTER VII

Ischemic Heart Disease

Atherosclerosis is the pathological process by which the structure of an artery is disrupted through the deposition of cholesterol with the intima of the wall. Initially starting as a "fatty streak" the accumulating cholesterol can lead to the formation of an atherosclerotic plaque with a more complex, but ultimately less stable, structure. During this process the endothelium becomes dysfunctional and the growing plaque can impinge on the lumen of the vessel causing reduced blood flow to the downstream tissue and cause ischemia. When the atherosclerotic plaque forms within the coronary arteries (coronary artery disease, or CAD), the subsequent myocardial ischemia can lead to acute coronary syndromes and ST segment elevation MI, or STEMI. When present in other circulations, atherosclerosis can contribute to stroke, peripheral arterial disease, aortic aneurysms, renal artery disease, and mesenteric ischemia.

The process by which atherosclerotic plaques form is summarized in figure 7.1, but there are four fundamental stages:

1.Endothelial cell injury. The process is likely initiated by endothelial damage. The potential causes of this damage are numerous and involve any toxin to which the endothelium is exposed. This is reflected in the risk factors for CAD such as tobacco use, diabetes, and dyslipidemia, all of which can cause endothelial damage. As well as chemical insults to the endothelium, excessive physical force can also cause damage and likely contributes to the correlation of CAD and hypertension.

2.Lipoprotein deposition. The damaged endothelium allows entry of cholesterol (LDL) into the vessel wall, whereupon it is oxidized (mLDL) and results in an inflammatory response that includes expression of MCP-1 (monocyte chemattractant protein-1) that attracts monocytes from the bloodstream. The monocytes enter the wall, and the mLDL promotes their transition to macrophage. The macrophages ingest the mLDL to become "foam cells" that form the fatty streak.

3. Inflammatory reaction. As well as consuming the mLDL, the macrophages release cytokines that attract other white blood cells (including T-lymphcytes) to the vessel wall through endothelial expression of adhesion molecules (e.g., ICAM-1, VCAM-1, E-selectin, and P-selectin).

4.Smooth muscle cell cap formation and weakening. The T-lymphocytes release cytokines that promote migration of smooth muscle cells to the surface of the plaque that create a "fibrous cap." This cap is initially thick and therefore stable. However, continued arrival and action of T-lymphocytes subsequently weaken the plaque's structural integrity as they penetrate the cap and release IFN-y that inhibits collagen production, while activated macrophages simultaneously destroy the cap's collagen. Calcification of the plaque also reduces its integrity. The weakened plaque is now more prone to rupture and inducing formation of a thrombus

Types of Myocardial Ischemia and Infarction

The degree of occlusion caused by the plaque and the oxygen demand of the myocardium determine the degree of ischemia that can develop. Arterial occlusion tends not to be a significant factor until the lumen is occluded by about 70 percent. Vascular occlusion may also be masked by formation of anastomoses (new vessels that bypass the occlusion). Rupture of the plaque and formation of a thrombus can drastically and quickly reduce the lumen and blood flow. The degree and duration of ischemia determine the type of acute coronary syndrome that occurs and the clinical impact. Mild or brief ischemia can lead to angina pectoris with no permanent tissue damage, but when ischemia is prolonged then myocardial infarction becomes more likely, and significant changes in ECG and release of cardiac enzymes are seen.

Stable and unstable angina pectoris

While not considered an acute coronary syndrome, stable angina is pain associated with periods of myocardial ischemia, usually associated with exertion and an increase in myocardial oxygen demand that is unmeet because of insufficient tissue perfusion. The inadequate perfusion is most commonly caused by coronary artery disease (vessel occlusion). Stable angina is predictable and regular, and resolves when the myocardial oxygen demand is reduced (i.e., cessation of exercise).

Unstable angina is more serious and may be an unpredictable exacerbation of anginal pain that had previously been stable. It may occur at rest or lower than usual levels of exertion. Unstable angina is part of the acute coronary syndrome spectrum and may reflect rupture of a plaque that has led to thrombosis. The ECG in unstable angina may show hyperacute T-waves, flattening of the T-waves, inverted T-waves, and ST depression. Without the presence of myocardial damage, unstable angina is not associated with elevated cardiac enzymes (e.g., troponin). Continued or worsening stenosis of the coronary artery leads to tissue infarction and more clinically significant elements of acute coronary syndrome.

Non-ST segment elevation myocardial infarction

With non-ST segment elevation myocardial infarction (NSTEMI), there is necrosis of the myocardium. Although, as the name suggests, there is no consistent ST segment elevation in a NSTEMI, other ECG changes may be seen. These include transient ST elevation, ST depression, or new T-wave inversions. The lysing myocytes release their contents including enzymes that can be used as biomarkers of the necrotic event. Presence of elevated cardiac enzymes distinguishes NSTEMI from unstable angina, but denotes myocardial damage and a poorer prognosis. There are several cardiac enzymes that can be detected (myoglobin, creatine kinase, and troponin I), and each has a different timeline from onset of infarction . But because of improvements in test sensitivity, the test enzyme of choice is troponin I.

Troponin

Troponin I is a normal protein important in the contractile apparatus of the cardiac myocyte. It is released into the circulation about three to four hours after MI and are still detectable for ten days afterward. The long half-life allows for the late diagnosis of MI but makes it difficult to detect reinfarction (a major complication associated with new thrombus formation during stent placement). Although there are a number causes for troponin elevation unrelated to MI, troponin elevation is much more sensitive and specific than myoglobin and even creatine kinase.

ST segment elevation myocardial infarction

ST segment elevation myocardial infarction (STEMI) most often results from complete occlusion of a major epicardial vessel. The resultant myocardial infarction raises cardiac enzymes measured in the blood (as with NSTEMI), but is accompanied by an ST segment elevation on the 12-lead ECG. This is the most serious of the acute coronary syndromes.

Pathophysiology of a STEMI

The most common cause of a STEMI is rupture of an atherosclerotic plaque. The continued degradation and calcification of the fibrous cap results in it breaking and spilling its contents into the bloodstream. Tissue factor within the necrotic core instigates the coagulation cascade when it is exposed to the blood and a thrombus is formed and the vessel is occluded. Plaques rupture most frequently at their "shoulder," the thin peripheral edges where proteolytic and apoptotic activity are highest and mechanical forces are most effective. The tissue downstream from the occlusion experiences ischemia and then infarcts. The impact on cardiac function and output depends on the site and extent of the infarcted tissue. For example, if a significant section of the left ventricular wall is involved, then the fall in cardiac output may be catastrophic, or if the papillary muscles of a valve are included, the valve may become incompetent and allow regurgitation.

Physical Exam of a STEMI

The physical examination findings may include elevated heart rate and blood pressure due to increased sympathetic tone. However, if cardiac function is severely impacted because of the size or location of the infarction, cardiogenic shock may result with a fall in blood pressure. The insufficient ATP production in the ischemic region means the interaction of actin and myosin in the cardiac myocytes cannot be broken and the muscle cannot relax. An S4 heart sound (figure 7.4) occurs when the noncompliant, stiffened left ventricle vibrates when blood enters from the atrium. The S4 sound is also known as an atrial gallop—not because the sound comes from the ventricle, but because it is associated with atrial contraction (and ventricular filling). If the infarction involves an impact of the papillary muscle function, the associated valve will fail and the regurgitation will cause a holosystolic murmur. A STEMI in the left ventricle sufficient to cause congestion and a rise in left-ventricular and end-diastolic pressure can lead to rises in left atrial and pulmonary pressure; this may be heard on the lung exam as rales due to the transient pulmonary edema.

Diagnosis of a STEMI

As mentioned above the two most important tools for diagnosing a STEMI are the ECG and the presence of cardiac enzymes that have been released into the bloodstream. Figure 7.4 shows the time line of myoglobin, creatine kinase, and troponin elevations after an infarction. Using the values of all three enzymes allowed the history of an infarction to be generated, but amazing improvements in the sensitivity of the troponin I test have allowed it to become the gold standard because of its specificity to the myocardium.

Changes in ECG

The first ECG sign to arise during a STEMI are "hyperacute T-waves" (figure 7.5). These T-waves are taller than normal and caused by the release of intracellular potassium from lysing cells and the consequent hyperkalemia in the surrounding tissue. Hyperacute T-waves are not often seen clinically because they occur so early in the event and prior to the patient's arrival in the hospital. Subsequent ECG stages are more commonly observed, and these include the ST elevation.

Determining which ECG leads show the ST elevation allow for the location of the infarcted tissue to be determined and provide insight into which coronary vessel is effected. How the leads of a twelve-lead ECG relate to the coronary vessels is summarized in figure 7.6. The following looks at the characteristic ECG changes in relation to location in a bit more detail (tip: relate back to figure 7.6 as you read the next sections).

Anterior wall myocardial infarctions (AWMI)

The anterior wall is affected when the left anterior descending coronary artery becomes occluded. Additional involvement of lateral and septal regions is indicative of the left main coronary artery being involved. Inclusion of these regions is termed an extensive anterior infarction. The ECG shows ST segment elevation in leads V3 and V4 (the anterior leads), seen as a raised J-point (see figure 7.7). A reciprocal ST depression will be seen in leads II, III, and aVF (the inferior leads). If the extent of the infarction is large, the elevated ST segment may been seen in the lateral and septal leads. The elevated ST segment is also associated in a change in shape of the T-wave as it becomes broader and loses its concave shape on the downward section. This broad T-wave can be higher as well as the ST elevation progresses, and its height can surpass the R-wave. These morphological changes result in a T-wave that looks like a tombstone.

Inferior wall myocardial infarction (IWMI)

Occlusion of the right coronary artery is the usual culprit for an inferior wall myocardial infarction (IWMI), which may be severe enough to extend to posterior regions. The ECG findings of an acute inferior myocardial infarction (figure 7.9) will be an ST segment elevation in leads II, III, and aVF (the inferior leads) and reciprocal depression in lead aVL (a lateral lead); without the reciprocal depression in aVL, alternative causes of ST segment elevation in the inferior leads should be considered (e.g., pericarditis). Because the right coronary artery perfuses the SA node, bradycardia may occur. An inferior MI can have multiple potential complications, including cardiogenic shock, atrioventricular block, or ventricular fibrillation, and can be fatal..

Posterior wall myocardial infarction (PWMI)

Most posterior myocardial infarctions occur with occlusion of the posterior descending artery (which in most people is a branch of the right coronary artery); because of the shared supply, a posterior infarction is often accompanied by an IWMI. The ECG findings include ST segment elevation in V7–V9 (the posterior leads that are placed on the posterior axillary line, not shown in figure 7.11) and ST depression in V1–V4 (the septal and anterior leads, shown in figure 7.10). If an IWMI is also present then there will be an ST elevation in leads II, III, and aVF (the inferior leads). A twelve-lead ECG showing a posterior wall infarction

9 798886 843255

Printed by Libri Plureos GmbH in Hamburg,
Germany